TRADE WINDS

by

RANDLE MANWARING

Palancar

ISBN: 0-9643256-8-3

The Palancar Company Limited
111 East 80th Street, New York, NY 10021
E-mail: Twolowns@aol.com

ACKNOWLEDGMENTS

Acknowledgment is given that some of these poems were first accepted for publication in

Oxford Poetry Quarterly, Contemporary Review, Poetry Nottingham, Pennine Platform, Iota, Hymn Society Bulletin, Sussex Express, Chichester Magazine, Acumen, Ore, Envoi, Outposts, Weyfarers, Poetry South East 2000, Vigil, Sing With Praise (Harper Collins), The Times Book of Prayers (Cassell) and *The Frogmore Papers.*

If thou indeed derive thy light from Heaven,
Then, to the measure of that Heaven-born light,
Shine, Poet! in thy place, and be content:
The stars pre-eminent in magnitude,
And they that from the zenith dart their beams,
(Visible though they be to half the earth,
Though half a sphere be conscious of their
    brightness),
Are yet of no diviner origin,
No purer essence, than the one that burns,
Like an untended watch-fire, on the ridge
Of some dark mountain; or than those which
    seem
Humbly to hang, like twinkling winter lamps,
Among the branches of the leafless trees.

William Wordsworth

CONTENTS

III

I

TRADE WINDS

They march across the oceans,
gentle in their attack
but not for trade or commerce
beat a track.

With north or south giving
direction to easterlies,
constant speed and power
embrace the breeze.

You may remain in doldrums
with much left to prove
or be caught up in the trade
winds of love.

UNFINISHED BUSINESS
- MARRIAGE

There are some who should be
and many who would be,
some who should not be
yet, those who are, entered
with highest hopes.

Honeymoons are always brief
some unexpectedly very
and even those who co-habit
find the eventual not
quite what they hoped for.

On our faces we write the story,
elation, contentment, pain;
unreturning, unremitting
years become explicit
and cannot be undone.

It is nature's festival,
a shower of stars, the fact
of two becoming one,
the romances of youth
outshining other loves.

In the tear-stained troughs,
or sun-drenched uplands,

in heart, mind and will
souls blend in unconscious
making and mending.

All earthbound pleasures are found
somewhere in the marriage bond,
friendship high on the agenda,
bodies expressively giving
their answers in the yes and no.

But whatever the exhilaration
of love in earthly form,
strawberries and cream
will be surpassed
in an unbelievable other life.

No longer a need to preserve
the human race, they neither
marry nor are given in marriage,
the communion of all souls,
as angels, incorruptible.

IMPERATIVES

Love is all,
     friendship nearly;
missing both
     we suffer dearly.

KEEPSAKE

This is a prayer I must not pray –
That on some glorious, autumn day
    You'll care for me.

WHAT IS A WOMAN?

What is a woman
-as if you didn't know -
splendidly different
    from the rest of the human.

Don't flinch if I mention
physical glory,
the golden casket
    contoured to perfection.

Indefinable soul,
heart, mind and will
conspire to make
    a mysterious whole.

Most taciturn,
the spirit's fire
incandescent,
    to warm or burn.

CLOTHES

If you merely like someone you may notice
what they are wearing but, more than that,
      every stitch.
Idiosyncrasies, too, will please
or infuriate depending on
      which is which.

SCRAPS

If you live on scraps
you will not starve
    and tasty morsels
    coming your way
may nourish your soul.

On the other hand,
those very pathetic
    protruding bones
    await a meal
to flesh them out.

UNSPOKEN

I had a dream
but not at night.
The vision came
though nothing seen.
Oh, just a thought
that comes and goes.

FEATURES

You can find them in little faces -
a smile, eyes, nose, from a mother,
hereditary likeness passing through
one generation to another.

Genes do their quiet genetic work
to bring about heredity,
the marvel of creation's
miraculous identity.

No two snowflakes are alike.

SINGLE PARENT

Young and beautiful,
she gave him love -
nothing more -
through childhood
and teenage years.
He does not look back
or on with anxiety;
his constant security
is all he knows.

UNDERSTANDING THE ART

It is not an exact science,
so do not allow those simple facts
        you know so well
to darken thought. Poets see
things somewhat differently
        and so they write.

Poems have several meanings and some
you will not fathom, though one perhaps
        is just for you.
If you found nothing, you might believe
a poet saw a visionary gleam
        he could not interpret.

POEMS

There is more to poetry than poetry;
for example, the type-face of the poem
and, most important, of its title.

Ideally, each poem needs space
but, at least, at top and tail,
with the poet's name correctly spelt.

The quality of paper helps a lot
and the style of the journal
whose editor publishes the best.

THE CULTURE OF POETS

They revel in geography,
with or without the maps,
loving the poetry of place,
Wessex and Wenlock Edge,
East Coker and Winander,
poets and their work
      reverberating
      in whispering cadences.

Also, they will understand
history in the round,
noting the tapestry
of world designs in
emergent or declining
nationhood,
      marked by the years
      of benison and blight.

So, poets will listen
to mankind's sad music,
the mystery and majesty
of personality,
wrestling against the odds
of privation and death.
      A few get special care,
      overwhelmingly loved.

II

AT THOMAS HARDY'S COTTAGE
Higher Bockhampton, Dorset

In his remote woodland home
poetry flourished within the soul
of Thomas Hardy; his earliest themes
laden with rhythm and cadences -
      Under the Greenwood Tree and
      Far from the Madding Crowd.

Although Wessex tales flowed freely
from his pen for many decades,
poetry he had always written
and when, in middle life, most hurt
      by those who hated Jude
      went back to writing poems.

Even the robin's song will falter
as midsummer grows silent
but Hardy gave his full song-cycle
in age when, sad but strong he left
      the harsh malignancy
      of Tess of the D'Urbervilles.

COTSWOLD IDYLL

Not hills in any real sense,
Cotswolds gently undulate,
dry-stone walls, limestone houses
with age hardening to gold.

Windrush's clear, bright stream
flowing through Bourton-on-the Water
near Risingtons, Great, Little and Wyck
past Slaughters, Lower and Upper.

Stow-in-the-Wold at the centre,
Nortons, Chipping and Over,
Evenlode quietly passing
Edward Thomas's Adelstrop.

Northward to Moreton-in-Marsh
where once four counties met -
Gloucestershire, Worcestershire,
Warwickshire and Oxfordshire.

Fairford, Bibury and Burford,
Northleach and north to Broadway
with Campdens, Chipping and Broad -
a canvas of England's heart.

TED HUGHES

In the high summer of her days
a Fulbright girl from Boston, Mass.
perished alone in Primrose Hill.

A few years later another died,
Assia gassed, embracing child;
the vestiges of further love.

Birthday Letters tell the story
with the Oedipal love of Daddy
and his, enigma from the egg.

AT THE RANDOLPH HOTEL, OXFORD

Drenched in academic bachelorhood,
the brothers sit waiting the end
of isolation. They know she may invade
the private world of Warnie and Jack
and that of Clive Staples Lewis.

The filming team have re-arranged
the furniture and changed the fitted carpets;
the stage is set for tea-time chatter
and Joy has come to greet her man,
who meets a joy as yet unmet.

Thus, into the years of *Shadowlands*
she steps to bring renaissance
to last from fifties into sixties,
her frank and forward ways to lift
her hero to undreamt fulfilment.

IN WESTMINSTER ABBEY
(At the Consecration of Bishop Ian Cundy, July 1992)

Happily for me, I was seated in Poets Corner
while Archbishop and Bishops moved into place
and the service proceeded with dignity and
    peace.

I glanced at the flagstones lying there, white
carved on black, noting the spread of fame
and the ages at which many poets had died.

Byron (in gold letters), the youngest to go,
D.H. Lawrence, later surviving his long trial
and Dylan Thomas, expiring in the U.S.A.

A short life for Jesuit, Gerard Manley Hopkins;
W.H. Auden with his flickering faith next
to John Masefield, (on a smaller stone), dying
    in age.

Writing light verse and some nonsense,
    Edward Lear
and Lewis Carroll, balanced up the cast,
William Blake in bronze surveying the scene.

Here was the ultimate spiritual mixture
of faith and doubt and every outrageous fortune -
song birds in the branches of an ancient tree.

ROBERT BURNS

*(thoughts from the Edinburgh Tattoo,
1996 - 200 years after his death)*

Sing the splendour of his songs,
poverty and passion joined,
a rural Don Juan becoming
the legendary Scottish bard.

Affection, love and marriage
in a life criss-crossing,
flowering in his poetry,
he lionized by society.

Praises and promises were mixed,
mirth, despair co-mingled;
fifes and pipes played gloriously
for Jean and him who loved.

SHAKESPEARE - ABRIDGED VERSION
(All 37 plays in 2 Hours - advert)

Cast away the cares of reading,
all the heavy-hearted learning,
all those complicated stories -
    everything is simplified.

Our greatest writer has been squeezed
through the literary pulp machine,
flattened on a single disc,
    every character cut down.

Hamlet close to *Julius Caesar,*
the *Dream, King Lear* and *The Merry Wives,*
Richard II and *Cymbeline,*
    drama - *As You Like It,* now.

ON SEEING PYGMALION
IN BERNARD SHAW'S GARDEN

The didactic spirit of a great dramatist
    moved in the evening air
while a middle-class audience for which he
  wrote
    was picnicking there.

Intellectual poverty which inspired him then
    survived in another age,
but the Fabian socialism he espoused
    still took the stage.

The Webbs and Annie Besant would have
  rejoiced,
    their phonetic friend still here
exposing moral and social evils
    without favour or fear.

Slum landlords have gone yet hardship lives on;
    still the poor have slender means,
New Socialism as helpless as other codes
    to deal with extremes.

Liza in apron and ostrich feathers,
    then changed by contrived education
to *My Fair Lady* outshining her mentors
    on *al fresco* location.

THE POET LAUREATE
(Andrew Motion)

Others excluded themselves
    without exception,
so the motion was carried
    with no objection.

TOMMY NUTTER
(1943 - 1992)

You were an artist in your time,
fancy waistcoats and two-tone suits.
So much you gave through London shops,
buyers admiring your artistry.

      A life foreshortened by tragedy
      casts an aura on your work;
      before research could find a cure
      you perished in your prime.

To-day I wear a dead man's suit,
a label bearing your famous name,
creations outliving the man who was
and us the men who wear them.

PARTING FROM BOOKS
(i.m. Professor Bonamy Dobrée, 1891-1974)

I'm getting rid of all my books,
you wrote; *not ill but getting old.*
I wondered then how you could leave
thousands of symbols of your past;
the books you wrote and one you shared
with him who fathered me, who did
research from which you slowly wrote,
in the thirties, *The Floating Republic.*

Your study lined with literature -
books reviewed, reference works.
Did you not keep back fifty or so
for reading in the hearthside chair,
your desert island in old age?
Later, a dozen for the bedside table,
old friends to cheer the final months;
finally some poems to hear, not see.

SHELF-LIFE

A, B and C, good men and true,
meet X, Y, Z (the opposite sex).

A quickly falls for Jenny Y
and, eventually, Z for C.

That leaves B on the shelf with X,
who do not click and mourn their fate.

They sidle, seared and frightened to
other rooms for some company.

The shelves are nearly empty and dark
but B finds there a mild flirtation.

X hears of this, comes over jealous
and goes berserk in a library.

TO A MANIC-DEPRESSIVE

Hullo, Pathetic, how are you to-day,
to-morrow or any day? Don't say.

Forget about that disfiguring mole
and adventure out of your boring hole,

your persona much less than it could be
as you fix on a supposed inadequacy.

I know you're gifted like the rest of us,
yet of your failures make an endless fuss.

You stand aloof, never willing to enthuse
and easy options continuously choose.

But wait, I see you cannot conceal
the pain of frustration you must feel,

I'm ashamed of my lack of empathy,
my judgement's superficiality.

FILMING A SOAP

A village within a village
where communities coalesce,
endlessly shooting scenes
programmed for television.

Here is a caravan with many
caravans together making one,
moving from pub to farm and back
in the ambit of the changing script.

A coach which serves as kitchen
stands cheek by jowl with another
as restaurant and a third
is ruled by the mistress of the robes.

A fitted coach for the make-up artist
next to one for the camera crew
and all their impedimenta; stationery
kept in boxes - nothing left to chance.

This fellowship gains popularity
shooting for hours to produce five minutes;
coach parties arriving to watch the filming,
later to watch in Barnsley and Hull.

Stars are given the best treatment,
tee-shirts and board games for emphasis,
producer, director and script-writer join
in stardom while the going is good.

EMPATHY

**(After reading James Kirkup's
Throwback - poems towards an Autobiography)**

For South Shields you could read South
    London
where, between the wars, it might have been
    me,
with father and mother loving me in poverty
in a street so little different in style.

The loneliness of a candle-lit bedroom,
deaths in the family presaging death
and other boys often wanting a fight
but always relations not far away.

My father a poorly-paid librarian,
making some extra from works of history,
I bored when helping with indexing;
he hoping I would follow in his steps.

The shops around the corner I knew well;
biscuits in tins and Golden Meadow butter,
and the place where I would buy the weekly
    pouch
of baccy for Dad and toffees for all.

The muffin man rang loudly with his bell,
the horse and cart brought traders down the road

and boys would gladly gather up the
  droppings,
selling it eagerly, but where, I never knew.

South London's poverty was thinly veiled,
six pounds of weekly wage bought just enough
but clothes came by another's generosity;
in all the North and South might empathise.

RITES OF PASSAGE - INDIA

BURNING THE OLD MAN

Fireworks flash in the night sky
while, marking the passing of the year,
      flames climb through a body of death.

The old man is burning quickly, feet first,
a figure of straw in something like
      the colours of Blackburn Rovers.

DAWN ELEPHANT RIDE

With confidence and grace
she places great feet
across the jungle path,
crushing bushes and branches
but, with the same legs,
fondles her young
with gentleness.

PRINCESSES AND PEERS

The Maharajah had a hundred wives
      so every other woman
         was a princess.
Similarly, Dissolution Honours
      spawn new Peers
         of uniform success.

SARAJEVO – 1914 - 1996

A pistol shot rang out in Sarajevo
and lights went out all over Europe.

Another war of death and homelessness
has blighted Bosnia and Hercegovina

but now the guns ringing that ancient city
fall silent as hope returns to Europe.

Never again will fleets and armies once
mobilised respond to Sarajevo.

III

TRIPLETS

Unremarkable, except as triplets,
they had a normal childhood,
doing their different things
     at home, at school.

One became a famous artist,
another ran a business,
the third became an Olympic
     gold medallist.

In later years, losing touch,
one day they decided to meet,
despite the crowds, in London
     at Victoria Station.

With no arrangements made on dress,
they were amused to find
they wore completely
     identical clothes.

GENETICS

Whenever I see a quiet crowd
of Japanese in Piccadilly,
I wonder if I helped to capture
a grandfather or two in 1944.

Apparently no ill effects
were passed on genetically,
although one feature still remains -
the height of visitors now and then.

CHANGES

When the bible came into English,
thousands of very religious people
mourned the loss of polysyllabic
Latin phrases long heard at Mass
and Hours. They much preferred the old.

When Isaac Watts wrote his hymns,
congregations thought them strange,
much preferring the metrical psalms
they knew so well. Anglicans at last
sang hymns, after the services.

Thomas Hardy gave us the picture
of Victorian life in the village church,
recalling the minstrels there providing
music to accompany all the singing.
The organ they thought rather modern
and it drove the musicians into the pub.

TREES IN SUMMER

Backdrop of summer days,
shield from heat, curtaining light,
splendour of variety, strength and song,
elm, ash and chestnut quietly join.

Rows of beeches crowd the view,
birches silvering monotony -
the earth's haphazard luxury
in woods of age and frailty.

Evergreens pine and fir
stabilise deciduousness,
while oaken ruggedness displays
quintessential Englishness.

Blackthorn, hawthorn decorate
with elderflower in mad profusion;
then the Burnet rose comes on,
embellishing midsummer days.

Sycamore and plane trees crowd
landscapes with too many leaves;
the rarer gentleness of larch
softens overbearing green.

Hornbeam and juniper add their styles,
yew and willow startlingly different
in the wild and quiet magnificence
of trees through summer's transience.

OCTOBER SONG

Revel in October days
shortening the calendar,
all things falling to the earth
     in death and fruitfulness.

Taste the last of summer's joys
in the new wine served as old,
breathe the softness of the south
     when migration calls.

Mark the cloudlets gentle shapes,
watch the slow, resurgent ploughing,
signs and hints of other days
     in the year's decline.

Stealthily the year descends,
hips and haws and yewberries
but sing a song of life at death
     in autumn's festival.

WHO WAS THERE?

At the literary prizegiving
I looked for the famous
poets, historians, novelists
    who were *not* there.

The up and coming ones,
the might have beens,
gathered literati -
    they were all there.

Right people won prizes,
the cameras flashed
and someone spoke wisdom
    to all of us there.

Then I met Donald Davie,
whose poems I liked -
in a very few minutes
    I was glad to be there.

VIOLENT SOCIETY

35,000 Taiwanese
visited us in '95,
fearlessly coming to London,
hazards no worse
than in the Orient.

Americans don't come
so often now; why should
they die by our bombs
when they can so easily
get murdered in New York.

HUNTING IS WITH THE BELVOIR
(From an estate agent's particulars).

A substantial country estate,
once the home of the Earl of Tiffany,
thirty bedrooms, usual offices,
billiards, library, indoor swimming pool,
fitted carpets, servants quarters,
cottages – all in excellent repair

*and hunting is with the Belvoir.**

On the borders of Leicester and Lincoln,
the hounds have kennels at Grantham;
the Duke will supervise;
hereditary peers welcome;
the Treasurer runs the office,
the Castle inspires tradition,

*and hunting is with the Belvoir.**

* *(Pronounced Beaver)*

LODGE MEETING

He drove his cab through London streets,
a very poor day, no one about,
so he was looking forward to lunch
at the Lodge Meeting near his home.

Won't cost me much, twenty quid,
to go to Charities; one day I'll go
through the chair but to-day I'll leave
before the real proceedings start.

Others will be sent out before me;
can't think why they come except,
like me, their turn will come one day.
Oh forget the cab, I'm on my way.

RECESSION

This street was never rich but once
small shops enriched the neighbourhood;
now it mirrors the wider field
of a visionless economy.

Hardboard hides the old shopfronts
and grills forbid all customers,
masking the lost euphoria
with the hopelessness of to-day's trade.

Posters declaim the latest Rock
or meetings of the local occult,
lending a hideous irony
to the pattern of failed enterprise.

The unreturning tide has gone
for many cold and silent moons;
driftwood and garbage strew the shore
for those who peer through whitewashed
    windows.

WHO GOES WHERE

(Arrangements have been made
for the re-positioning of bodies, when they die,
in some private graves)

Jim may now expect to lie
Where his brother was to be
but Jane must keep her distance
then and through eternity.

Shuffle half the living pack
so they can anticipate
better neighbours being dead
than at this early date.

CRICKETING COUNTIES

First-class cricketing counties
huddle together - the North, nearly
all Midlands, Greater London
and the West, leaving in the cold
Norfolk, Suffolk, Lincolnshire
      with far westerlies,
        Devon and Cornwall.

Coloured counties do well,
Northants and Worcestershire
like book-ends on Warwick,
plus Hants, Glamorgan and now,
in the far north, Durham.
      Who'll be the next
      to take centre stage?

SABINA PARK, KINGSTON, JAMAICA

In a cauldron of skill and passion
West Indian life is matched and mixed
for a cricket festival of grace and pace,
a fiery contest in tropic heat.

Children beg or jostle for work
and vendors vend relentlessly;
Heineken, Red Stripe and soft drinks,
peanuts, doughnuts, ice creams compete.

Oblivious to killings at the wicket,
vultures float on currents of air,
Blue Mountains surrounding in over sight,
impassioned in victory or defeat.

No place for faint hearts on the pitch
where matches are played in fierce combat;
the powerful and tall winning the day
in roles reversed from colonial days.

BRIEF CASES

Attaché cases were in vogue
for carrying sandwiches to work
with *The Daily Telegraph*
      between the wars.

Then, with bowler and umbrella
signalling successful city man,
came a new and suppler version
      after the war.

The zip appeared to slim things down
and briefs were neat or not at all;
perhaps the pink *Financial Times* -
      a phoney war.

Larger cases now exist
for taking filing systems around,
needing a strong-arm junior
      for the paper-war.

CREDIT

The girl in the bank
told me I looked smart.
I appeared to take no notice
    but I did.

The girl in the bank
worked her machine,
checking my account
    at least with them.

Vanity struts
in and out of the bank
I played my card for cash,
    remaining in credit.

NINE O'CLOCK NEWS

You switch on the News,
a moment or so late,
hearing a famous name
dynamically mentioned.

You think he has died
and, when another name
is joined, you wonder if both
have been bombed to death.

But soon you hear
that Nelson Mandela
and President De Klerk
have won the Nobel Prize
        – for Peace.

DROWNING OF KITTENS

A cupboard made ready for the birth
where she was happy in its warmth,
suckling the kittens, licking their fur -
this was a sight for children to enjoy.

But when, during the next day or so,
the babies were taken, wrapped in a cloth
and drowned in a bucket taken outdoors,
we felt the force of minor tragedy,

except that, usually, one kitten was spared
to satisfy maternal instinct;
some pity shown for feline feeling -
the impossible balance of joy and grief.

No tears were shed, accepting sadly
the inevitability of cruel death,
repeated each year monotonously,
reflecting life's greater tragedies.

CORMORANTS

While cormorants perch and fish,
fish and fly in slow routine,
waves fall in animation,
lightening the darkness.

BLUE WHALES

For fifty million years
you flourished in the unknown
        world of water,
singing your mating songs
across the ocean beds
        through thousands of miles.

Once, explosive harpoons
tried to eliminate
        our largest creature
but now, in Californian seas,
you feed and frolic in lives
        of pastime and passion.

IV

WORKING THROUGH
DISAPPOINTMENTS

LORD GOD, you know they seemed so great -
those many disappointments and frustrations
    which I met when hopes were high
    but now I see them as just part
of a detailed plan for me.

I cannot tell what tomorrow holds
of joy and laughter, pain and tears
    but offer thanks for what is past
    and when some things come back to haunt
I clasp the hand of one who knows the way.

DARKNESS
(I am not silenced by the darkness - Job ch.23 v.17)

Dead Bird in the Psyche

Trapped in the chimney, struggling,
churning out dirt, dust and soot,
detritus of its own making,
it died
but in its living death
distils hatred, deviously made,
odious, odorous, sinister.

February

It is the blackest month,
the hour before the dawn;
earth lies leafless, seemingly
dead and derelict;
though, soon a resurrection
from the tomb of the year
will release hopeful,
burgeoning life.

FORTY DAYS

Will He be coming to dine to-night -
    the King to speak of His Kingdom
      in the years to come?

We must not miss His next appearance
    in that newly glorified body
      we have grown so used to.

What fresh truth will He give us when
    He joins us for a meal
      sharing our joy?

We must prepare for another day
    when we are without Him,
      facing the world.

A DEAD CHURCH

Ivy on the notice board
and a solitary bell
hangs outside the darkened building.

A drooping clanger hanging loose
as life and song have vanished from
a house once full of singing.

WHEN GOD
BECAME OUR NEIGHBOUR

"Whatever you did for one of the least of these brothers of mine, you did for me".

Matthew 24.40

When God became our neighbour
in coming down to earth,
He took the name of Jesus
at His humble birth.
He always cared for others,
the lonely and the sad;
the helpless and the cripples
in meeting Him, were glad.

He told us that in seeking
for others in their need,
we give to Him devotion
in every loving deed.
So help us to be active
in coming to the aid
of those who will be feeling
most worried and afraid.

Release from fear and sadness
the house-bound and the old,
the prisoners of ageing
in our lives enfold;
and may the Lord's compassion

He comes to us to prove,
bind young and old together
in life-enriching love.

(Written as a hymn at the request of Help the Aged*)*

THE MILLENNIUM

Two thousand years have come and gone,
vanished like the morning mist,
since he entered the world he made,
God's only son, both Lord and Christ.
      Two thousand years but as two days
      with him to whom we offer praise.

Two thousand years of peace and war,
holding the nations in their grip,
with man's inhumanity to man
marking mankind's membership.
      Two thousand years but as two days
      with him to whom we offer praise.

Two thousand years of history,
leaders and despots, kings and queens,
empires rising, at length to fall,
unable to find survival's means.
      Two thousand years but as two days
      with him to whom we offer praise.

Two thousand years' inventiveness,
frontiers pushed forward constantly
but man, poor King over his nature,
dragging life down most wantonly.
      Two thousand years but as two days
      with him to whom we offer praise.

Two thousand years of the Christian church,
always growth and always decay,
with many a stain upon her dress,
the blood of the martyrs marking the way.
　　Two thousand years but as two days
　　with him to whom we offer praise.

A CENTURY OF WAR

A world hierarchy
of blood-lust and strutting power
governed all the low decades –
Boers and the blood baths
on the battlefields of France
    to end war.

Fascism and communism locked.
Hiroshima and Nagasaki
followed the holocaust;
later Korea and Vietnam
plunged into bitter conflict
    and hopeless war.

Pol Pot and Khmer Rouge
slaughtered in Cambodia;
a six-day fight in Israel,
a Timananmen massacre,
plus Gulf and Bosnia gripped
    in local war.

Africa decolonised
but soon aflame, north
south, east and west,
Serbia ringing down a curtain
on a hundred years,
    to end war?

ULSTER REMEMBERED

In the streets of Londonderry,
walking of a Sunday afternoon,
boys called out in unison –
    dirty British, dirty British.

In the Eglinton post office,
buying stamps in war-time,
a lady said the crops were bad –
    the British are here, the British are here.

THEY HAVE NO WINE
(St. John Ch. 2 Verse 3)

Surviving every merger,
fat cats predominate,
multiplying profits,
scything down the work force.
Millionaires ten a penny,
raffling Rolls Royces,
Formula 1 leading,
amusing ourselves to death.

Treading the shopping malls
buying till we drop
in unwanted spending
backed by plastic debt,
headlong we travel
at a quickening pace
with everything yet nothing
and we have no wine.

FOR DAVID AND SALLY
(Married 25th October, 1997)

Time, to-day, stands still
yet clocks go back awhile
to when you were with us,
those many years ago.

It is as if your youth
is born again, renewed
out of the storehouse
of all your yesterdays.

The intervening years
as not discounted as
part of the plan for both
in life's deep mystery.

So, let there be rejoicing
with them, beloved and loving,
whose lives now come together
in love's returning spring.

JANICE JONES (1945-1999)

Wired to ease the pain
she sat upright
as if there were no threat,
then, drifting in and out
of consciousness, she faced
the awesome foe
so recently encountered.

Everything she touched
and everyone
was with her love;
gentle and giving,
she learned that touch
from One who made her heart
and all hearts to be loved.

Do not grieve for her
whose life, though brief
was complete
and now her seraph spirit,
freed from the pain,
puts on another suit,
immortal, for ever Janice.

LEWES, EAST SUSSEX

Lewes is the most romantic situation I ever saw
Daniel Defoe

History has made this narrow street –
Protestant martyrs and rebel leader –
but now, in English hopefulness,
shops endure vagaries of trade.

Mister Chips and *Full of Beans,*
Lucy of Lewes – everything home-made,
Capriccio and *Elegance* for ladies,
club-ties for gentlemen in *Hugh Rae.*

Fifteenth century bookshop takes pride
while *Marston-Barrett* spreads his gems,
joining skills of the horologist
in service and culture of the County Town.

Further east the pervading Law Courts
face the ageless *White Hart Hotel*
where Tom Paine led his *Headstrong Club*
but managed to marry a Lewes girl.

PREVIOUS PUBLICATIONS

POETRY

Posies Once Mine (Fortune Press)	*(1951)*
Satires And Salvation (Mitre Press)	*(1960)*
Under The Magnolia Tree (Outposts)	*(1965)*
Slave To No Sect (Mitre Press)	*(1966)*
* Crossroads Of The Year (White Lion)	*(1975)*
* From The Four Winds (White Lion)	*(1976)*
In A Time Of Unbelief (Henry Walter)	*(1977)*
* Thank You, Lord Jesus (Henry Walter)	*(1980)*
The Swifts Of Maggiore	
(Fuller D'arch Smith)	*(1981)*
In A Time Of Change	
(Coventry Lanchester Polytechnic)	*(1983)*
Collected Poems (Charles Skilton)	*(1986)*
Some Late Lark Singing (Brentham Press)	*(1992)*
Love So Amazing (Ikon)	*(1995)*

PROSE

The Heart Of This People (Quaintance)	*(1954)*
A Christian Guide To Daily Work (Hodder)	*(1963)*
Thornhill Guide To Insurance (Thornhill)	*(1976)*
The Run Of The Downs (Caldra House)	*(1984)*

From Controversy To Co-Existence
(Cambridge University Press)   *(1985)*
The Good Fight (Howard Baker Press)   *(1990)*
A Study Of Hymnwriting
And Hymnsinging In The
Christian Church (Edwin Mellen Press)   *(1991)*
* The Swallows, The Fox And The Cuckoo   *(1997)*

(M. and N. Publications)

* For Children

When visiting Robert Frost country in Vermont, Randle Manwaring was introduced, with some hyperbole, as being *like our Wallace Stevens, an Insurance Executive by vocation and a poet by avocation.* Years earlier, Randle had met Walter de la Mare who, at a never to be forgotten tea party, gave him expert guidance and encouragement with his juvenilia. In fact, this present volume is the fourteenth to appear since the initial publication nearly fifty years ago.

Several poems have been set to music, one by Louise Denney and performed by several Guards bands in the U.K., for example in Bath and Battle Abbey. At the other end of the scale, a poem appeared on London buses and readings have been given on television channels, in clubs, pubs and schools.

Randle Manwaring, at one time a managing director of a firm of Lloyds insurance brokers, was President of the Society of Pension Consultants and then chairman of two boarding schools, at one later teaching poetry to dyslexic children. For a number of years he was on the Bishop's Council in Chichester, Sussex where he continues to be a Diocesan Reader. In war time, Randle rose to the rank of Wing

Commander in the Royal Air Force and in 1945 relieved Japanese generals of their swords at a V.J. ceremony in Rangoon.

Randle Manwaring is married with four children, eleven grandchildren and several great grandchildren.